0s AND 40s BRITAIN

BY

JOHN GUY

COUNTRY LIFE

LAND ARMY

This view of a typical farming scene in the 1940s shows a woman taking part in the government's 'Women's Land Army' campaign. In the early years of the war, Britain faced both a food and labour shortage. Many farm labourers had joined the armed forces and women were encouraged to take their jobs.

There were two major events during the 1930s and 1940s that affected everyone in Britain. The Depression, which lasted from 1929 to the mid-1930s, and the Second World War (1939-45) created one of the worst periods in British history. The Depression caused misery in country areas, as well as in the great industrial towns in the north, and changes that happened then still affect country life today. There was a sudden fall in the price of grain on the world markets, which meant farmers could not make money by growing food crops. The second, and greatest change came during the war. The Germans stopped merchant ships from crossing the Atlantic Ocean which caused food shortages in Britain. Farmers were forced to use more intensive growing methods to meet the demand for food. This meant increased mechanization and, after the war, there were far fewer jobs in farming.

OLD WAYS

Before the Second World War, many of the traditional jobs on the farm were still performed by horse-power, such as ploughing. Today, heavy horses are usually only seen at special agricultural shows and are no longer a familiar part of the countryside.

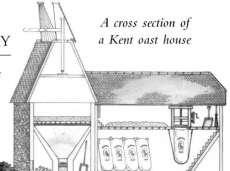

A cross section of a Kent oast house

Oast houses were once a familiar scene in the south-east. They were drying kilns for hops, grown for the brewing industry to make beer. Many Londoners from the East End spent their summer 'holiday' in Kent gathering in the hops, living in camps on the farms. Sadly, mechanization and cheaper imports meant the hop industry nearly disappeared. Most oast houses are now converted into private homes.

'DIG FOR VICTORY'

During the war the government introduced many special campaigns, with catchy slogans, to encourage people to work together to defeat the enemy. One of the most successful of these was the 'Dig for Victory' campaign, where people were encouraged to grow their own food. Allotments, introduced during the First World War, became common again and country people with larger gardens, were encouraged to grow as much food as possible to help overcome local food shortages.

THE KING VISITS

The mining valleys of south Wales were badly affected during the Depression as there was often no alternative work. In 1936, shortly before he abdicated, Edward VIII visited the valleys, and protested to the Government that *"… something must be done to find these people work."*

COUNTRY SPORTS

Traditional country sports such as shooting and fishing, were popular in the 1930s and 40s, especially during the war years when meat was rationed. They took part in organized shoots, while the poor caught wild rabbits to help feed their families..

LIFE IN TOWNS

CHEAP HOUSING

Most of the housing for the working classes was built in town centres, close to the factories and other places of industry. Some local authorities built houses which they rented out, but most working-class houses were built by private landlords, who rented the properties out for low weekly rents.

Although Britain was still suffering from the effects of the Depression throughout the 1930s, from about 1937 there were signs of improvement. As the heavier, more traditional industries of the north went into decline, the newer, lighter industries, such as the manufacturing goods of electrical, gradually began to grow. The better-off south-east felt less of the effect of the Depression and recovered quickest. By 1933 the National Grid had been completed, bringing electricity to those who could afford it, and most towns had tarmacked roads, to cope with the growing use of motor cars. Most towns also had their own gas works, providing lighting and heating to many homes.

BLACKOUTS

During the war everyone had to blackout all their windows at night with heavy curtains and blinds, so they did not present a target to German bombers. Street lamps and even vehicle head-lamps were forbidden, and special wardens patrolled the streets to make sure everyone obeyed.

SUBURBIA

The growing middle classes chose to live in the new suburbs that began to appear on the outskirts of the towns, and commute into the towns to work. Mostly employed in professional occupations, they could usually arrange a mortgage and buy their own houses, often for less than the working classes paid in rent. Semi-detached houses with gardens became popular at this time. A typical, three-bedroomed house in the 1930s cost between £400 and £500. It could be secured with a £5 deposit and weekly payments of just 60p–70p.

INDUSTRIAL POLLUTION

The Depression of the 1930s brought hardship to those who lived and worked in the heavily industrialized towns. Sheffield, shown here, was once the centre of the British steel industry. However, as such industries declined, many factories were demolished, making way for newer, cleaner industries.

HEALTH IMPROVEMENTS

Sanitation in towns improved greatly in the 1930s. By that time, all towns had a mains water supply and improved drainage systems, which reduced the number of water-borne diseases. Improved health care, such as iron lungs for polio sufferers (below right), and x-ray equipment, was also introduced.

NEW TOWN PLANS

German bombing campaigns of the Second World War had an unexpected effect on the townscapes of Britain in the years that followed. The first job was to clear up the mess, but then the towns had to be rebuilt. Many town centres owe their present open plans to this post-war rebuilding.

HAPPY MOTORING

During the 1930s motoring became very popular with the upper and middle classes. A typical small family car in 1935, such as the Austin 10 or Morris Minor cost around £120. These were the most popular cars in Britain at the time.

A PLACE IN THE SUN

Holidays abroad were popular with the rich – an escape from the gloom of the 1930s. The British-built *Queen Mary* had her maiden voyage in 1936. At that time she was the largest ocean-going liner and regularly crossed the Atlantic Ocean to New York.

'BRITAIN CAN MAKE IT'

At the end of the Second World War, British manufacturers launched a 'Britain Can Make It' exhibition, to show off the expertise of the new manufacturing industries. Many new designs and inventions were presented, such as this bicycle which had a dynamo and motor, suspension, shaft drive, electric bell and miniature radio. It was typical of the new ideas being developed at the time as Britain's factories switched from making weapons to luxury items.

ROYAL FAVOURITES

George VI and his wife, Elizabeth Bowes-Lyon, were amongst our most loved monarchs. They made themselves popular when they refused to leave England during the Second World War, even after Buckingham Palace itself was bombed in 1940. The royal family spent most of the war mainly in the Royal Lodge, in the grounds of Windsor Castle. Princess Elizabeth (the present queen) is shown second from the left.

LIFE FOR THE RICH

By the 1930s few middle-class families could afford servants, and even the upper classes reduced the number of staff they had. After the war ended, servant numbers stayed lower than in Victorian and Edwardian times. There were new, labour-saving machines that could be used easily. Most wealthy people did not experience the hardship of the Depression. Even during the war, the rich were able to buy the goods they needed on the 'black market'. However, many of their large houses were taken over by the armed forces at this time.

LIFE GOES ON

The rich enjoyed a fairly unchanged lifestyle throughout the difficulties of the 1930s and 40s. Most were office workers and were not affected by the worst aspects of the Depression. Many still enjoyed a busy social life with plenty of time for dances and functions.

THE HIGH LIFE

During the 1930s new ideas were introduced in interior design, using new materials such as chrome and Bakelite. This view of a sitting room in a typical middle-class home is quite like today's designs. Many wealthy people decorated their homes in the modern artistic styles, such as Art Deco.

THE POOR AT HOME

The poor were affected most by the Great Depression of the 1930s. Most were unskilled labourers who could not easily find work when factories closed down. The Depression began on 24 October 1929 when the New York Stock Exchange collapsed. The price of wheat in America suddenly fell, followed by most other goods. Many businesses and governments throughout the developed world lost fortunes. Unemployment rose rapidly throughout the next 10 years as Britain (and the world's) main industries collapsed. In 1936, unemployed ship builders from Jarrow (in north-east England), where nearly 80 percent of the workers were unemployed, marched to London to protest to the government.

MASS-PRODUCTION

This view shows men working on a production line in a car assembly factory in Oxford, around 1930. Many traditional industries, such as ship building, coal mining and steel works, were in trouble after the Depression. Many men had to take unskilled work in factories earning, in the late 1930s, about £400 per year.

CHEAP DAY RETURN

Most poor people could not afford holidays. Most men worked a six-day week and few jobs paid holiday money. When they could afford it, working-class families might go to the local beach on a day trip. They usually travelled by train.

BARMOUTH NORTH WALES
FOR MOUNTAIN, SAND & SEA
Illustrated Guide 6d., Heulwen Tourist Office, Barmouth
TRAVEL BY TRAIN BRITISH RAILWAYS

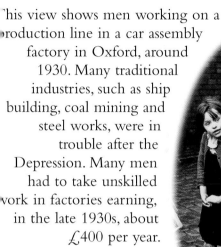

THE GREAT DEPRESSION

The effects of the Depression were felt for the next 10 years and only really came to an end at the outbreak of the Second World War. The main problem was mass-unemployment. By the mid-1930s unemployment reached three million in Britain, the highest ever recorded. The unemployed received some financial help from the government – about £1.50 a week per family. Jobs were often given out on a daily basis, and workers had to queue at factory gates each morning in search of work.

POOR PAY

Another major effect of the Depression was the reduction in wages, caused by a smaller demand for goods. Working conditions also worsened and some workers went on strike for better pay and conditions. Strikers received no pay and only a little support from the unions, so most workers would only strike as a last resort. Because so many people were looking for jobs, some bad employers deliberately kept wages low and threatened to sack strikers, offering their jobs to the unemployed.

BASIC ACCOMMODATION

Most working-class homes were rented, usually from private landlords. There was little spare money for luxuries, as most of the wages were spent on food and rent. Many poorer families still cooked on open ranges. The lucky ones had small gas cookers, like this one, which were more efficient.

DRIED FOOD

Another method of food preservation that gained popularity at this time was dehydration. The liquid content of foods such as mashed potato and eggs (shown above) is withdrawn and the remaining food powdered. It is reconstituted by simply adding water. Powdered egg was a main ingredient during the war years.

COFFEE BLENDS

Coffee first appeared in England in the 17th century but, for a long time, it was an expensive luxury. In Britain coffee has always been less popular than tea, but by the 1930s companies such as Lyons, offered a range of blends. The beans were mostly from Africa and South America. During the war, when coffee was scarce, alternatives were introduced, such as roasted chicory roots. Instant coffee was first marketed in America in 1937.

THE COMMON MAN'S DRINK

It was around 1930 that tea stopped being a luxury and became more easily available to all. Tea production had increased throughout the empire. Tea, mainly from India and China, soon became the most popular drink of the working classes.

INCREASED YIELDS

Until the late 1930s the only form of crop fertilizer was manure and other organic matter. During the food shortage of the war however, scientists developed chemical fertilizers that helped to increase crop yields. The first fertilizers were used in 1940, and by 1944 they were widely used.

FOOD AND DRINK

*D*uring the Second World War the Germans mounted a U-boat campaign against the allied merchant ships. This caused great food shortages. The British and American governments then put an enormous amount of money into food technology research. New techniques were developed to preserve food, and safe chemicals were added to food to make it better for us. It was believed that a hungry country would not be able to fight properly against the Germans. This work formed the basis of today's high-technology food industry.

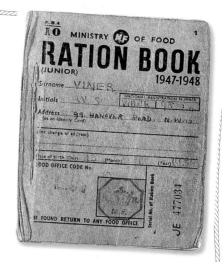

RATIONING

Rationing had first been introduced during the First World War. It was introduced again in 1940. Coupons had to be presented when buying items such as food, clothing and petrol. Queues became a part of life, with people trying to make sure they got their share before supplies ran out. Rationing continued after the war; clothes became unrationed in 1949 but food remained on ration until 1954. If you were invited to dine at someone else's house, it was usual to take your rations with you, rather than eat your host's food.

PROCESSED FOODS

Scientists involved in food technology during the war greatly improved the methods used for drying and canning food. Processed food could be stored safely for long periods, often with the addition of chemicals to prevent mould growth.

PASTIMES

*D*uring the Depression, few could afford to spend much time and money on enjoyable pastimes. However, in following years, although times were hard, people began to have more fun. During the Second World War, many people took a 'live for the moment' approach to life, as they never knew if they were going to be bombed and die. They enjoyed going to the cinema, the pub and the local dance hall as well as listening to the radio. After the war British seaside resorts reopened. Many had been closed to the public but now they began to thrive again.

RADIO

By the 1930s radio was one of the most popular forms of home entertainment. The BBC provided a range of programmes including music, news, comedy and talk shows. Families regularly sat around the radio listening to serial stories. King Edward VIII announced his abdication over the radio in 1936, and on 3 September 1939 the Prime Minister, Neville Chamberlain, announced that Britain was at war with Germany.

THEATRE GOING

A lot of entertainment was live. People enjoyed going to the theatre and every town in Britain could usually boast at least one – and often several – theatres, showing anything from comedy to serious drama. Music Hall was also very popular. As films became more popular, many theatres closed down after the 1940s or were converted into cinemas.

A DAY AT THE RACES

Horse-racing was popular with the middle and upper classes, and the working classes enjoyed dog-racing. During the Second World War however, less sport was played. This was partly because many of the sports grounds were used for other things. The Oval cricket ground, for example, was used as a prisoner-of-war camp.

A NIGHT AT THE 'FLICKS'

Theatre and cinema provided an escape from reality. Sometimes shows and films had to be staged during the day because of blackout restrictions. Cinemas regularly had audiences of 25–30 million each week. Favourite were Hollywood movies, such as *The Wizard of Oz*, which starred Judy Garland and was the first film produced in Technicolor. The British film industry was also active at this time, mainly making morale-boosting wartime dramas. Cinemas also showed up-to-date newsreel films which gave people an idea of how the war was going.

FIRST TELEVISION SERVICE

Television was a new and exciting form of entertainment in the 1930s, although only the very rich could afford one and broadcasts were limited. During the war, programmes stopped altogether. Equipment used to transmit the signal (and even the television sets themselves) was huge. This view shows the first television station at Alexandra Palace. The world's first television service was broadcast in 1936 by the BBC.

THE LIGHT FANTASTIC

A popular pastime for people of all classes was dancing. Ballroom dancing was very popular, but around this time modern dancing began to appear. Young couples danced to swing and jazz bands. Many of the musicians were serving military bandsmen who entertained the armed services abroad, or civilians when at home on leave. One of the most popular dance crazes of the early 1940s was the Jitterbug, brought over from America.

FASHION

Clothing became much brighter during the 1930s until the start of the Second World War. Women's clothes became very elegant. New types of fasteners, such as zips and press-studs, made it easier to dress and undress, and dress designers developed new designs because of these. For the first time, there were lots of different styles, and women were able to dress how they wished. More colours were used, even for men who now wore pastel-coloured shirts instead of the more usual white. Hollywood had a great influence on fashion at this time, too. Many men tried to copy the styles of the great film stars.

HAIRSTYLES

By the 1930s, short bobs were often replaced with long, wavy hair, often permed into curls. For men, hair dressings in the form of oils and creams to create a smooth, swept-back look became fashionable.

SHEER ELEGANCE

Before the invention of nylon in 1935, stockings were usually made of expensive materials such as silk. Nylon, an artificial material, was very popular, but was in short supply during the war years. Stockings at that time had a seam running up the back of the leg and it became fashionable for women to paint a black line up the back of their legs to imitate nylon stockings.

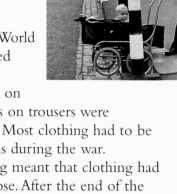

PLAIN AND PATRIOTIC

During the Second World War it was considered unpatriotic to waste money and resources on fashion. Even turn-ups on trousers were replaced with plain legs. Most clothing had to be bought using clothing coupons during the war. Shortages of cloth and rationing meant that clothing had to be practical and multi-purpose. After the end of the war, most people enjoyed wearing more colourful and fashionable clothes, when most of the earlier styles of the 1930s came back.

MAKING DO

During the war, people were encouraged to make do with the clothing they had and mend it rather than replace it. People were asked to make their own clothes from recycled materials, using pattern books, as shown above. Most clothing was plain and practical, with no added details.

FOOTLOOSE

During the early 1930s there were some quite extraordinary new designs in footwear, especially for ladies, such as platform soles and wedge heels. During the war years shoes became more practical and were designed for comfort rather than elegance. The government encouraged people to repair their old shoes rather than waste valuable resources buying new ones.

ART AND ARCHITECTURE

*D*uring the war people became much more interested in the arts. The government set up the Council for the Encouragement of Music and the Arts (CEMA), which after the war became known as the Arts Council. Theatre, ballet and classical music tours around the country were sponsored to take art to the people. Concerts organized for the troops and war workers were very popular. Some of the larger towns outside London (such as Bournemouth and Birmingham) began their own symphony orchestras, which still exist today. The most popular style in art and design was Art Deco. It has greatly influenced many modern styles with its bold, practical yet imaginative styles.

BENJAMIN BRITTEN
(1913–76)

One of the most popular British composers of the time was Benjamin Britten, who revived interest in opera with *Peter Grimes* and other pieces. He also composed a number of works for children, including *The Young Person's Guide to the Orchestra*.

ARCHITECTURE

RECEPTION OFFICE

Before the war the main styles in architecture were Art Deco and Modernist. Art Deco was used for larger buildings, such as the amazing Hoover building (left). Modernist buildings were made of concrete, steel and glass, and they were very practical. After the war, new housing estates and town centres had to be planned. The first high-rise buildings were designed using steel girders and reinforced concrete. This meant the floors carried the strength of the buildings instead of the walls.

SOMERSET MAUGHAM

William Somerset Maugham (1874-1965) was a great English novelist, playwright and short-story writer, who was writing a lot at this time. His style of writing has been described as 'realist' and included such works as *Of Human Bondage* and *The Moon and Sixpence.*

HENRY MOORE (1898-1986)

Henry Moore was commissioned to paint a series of pictures to illustrate the effect of the Second World War on Britain. He chose subjects such as the cramped living conditions in the underground stations of London, which were used as bomb shelters. He is more famous today for his unusual style of sculpture. This statue, called *Composition,* was produced for the 'Art for the People Exhibition'.

HEALTH AND MEDICINE

*T*n 1948 the National Health Service was introduced. It was the first fully state-funded health service in the world. Before that the level of care given to patients depended on where they lived and what they could afford. The government now paid for health care through taxes, and made sure that everyone received the same level of care. They also controlled the training of doctors and nurses. After this change, standards in health care and medical research improved greatly.

X-RAYS

The discovery of x-rays was made by Wilhelm Röntgen in 1895. It was used to take 'photographs' of the inside of the body. Doctors could then make a diagnosis without having to perform surgery. By the 1930s, x-rays were also used to treat certain diseases such as cancer, some skin complaints and even ringworm.

PREVENTATIVE MEASURES

In the 1930s an education programme was launched to have children immunized against common, but serious, childhood illnesses, such as diphtheria, a throat infection that caused many deaths amongst children at this time.

HOSPITAL CARE

Before the introduction of the National Health Service, hospitals in Britain were owned and managed in one of three main ways: by local authorities; by a charity; or privately by a doctor, or group of doctors, for profit. The level of care varied enormously, not only between these three groups, but also according to where people lived. Poor, working-class areas had the worst health care, while the best was in the private hospitals.

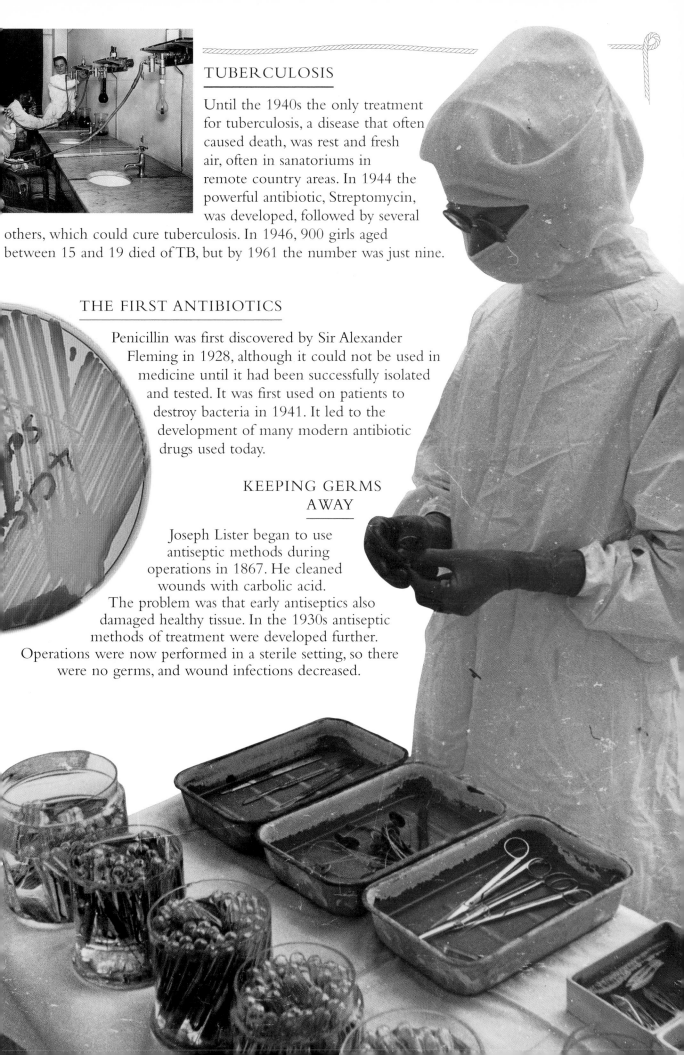

TUBERCULOSIS

Until the 1940s the only treatment for tuberculosis, a disease that often caused death, was rest and fresh air, often in sanatoriums in remote country areas. In 1944 the powerful antibiotic, Streptomycin, was developed, followed by several others, which could cure tuberculosis. In 1946, 900 girls aged between 15 and 19 died of TB, but by 1961 the number was just nine.

THE FIRST ANTIBIOTICS

Penicillin was first discovered by Sir Alexander Fleming in 1928, although it could not be used in medicine until it had been successfully isolated and tested. It was first used on patients to destroy bacteria in 1941. It led to the development of many modern antibiotic drugs used today.

KEEPING GERMS AWAY

Joseph Lister began to use antiseptic methods during operations in 1867. He cleaned wounds with carbolic acid. The problem was that early antiseptics also damaged healthy tissue. In the 1930s antiseptic methods of treatment were developed further. Operations were now performed in a sterile setting, so there were no germs, and wound infections decreased.

LOVE AND MARRIAGE

The Depression and the Second World War were very difficult times. Many people were unhappy and others 'lived for the moment', enjoying exciting, 'whirlwind' romances. This continued after the war, too, and is perhaps a reason why so many couples got married after they had only known each other for a short time. People began to feel that they did not have to accept things the way they had before. For example, some, who were in unhappy marriages, decided to leave their husband or wife. The divorce rate in Britain rose, and has been gradually increasing ever since.

ROMANTIC STORIES

Many women's magazines appeared around this time, telling stories of love and romance between men and women, often in exotic places. Many women from very poor backgrounds probably read the stories to cheer themselves up.

THE COST OF ROMANCE

One of the most famous love affairs in British history happened at this time. The future Edward VIII met and fell in love with an American, Mrs Wallis Warfield Simpson, on one of his many trips to America. She had already divorced one husband and was divorcing a second when she first met Edward in 1931. However, the Church of England would not allow a divorcée to be queen of England. As King, Edward would also be head of the English Church, so the romance caused a crisis. Even after his succession to the throne, Edward refused to give Wallis up. So, after just 325 days, he abdicated. Edward and Wallis Simpson left England for France, where they married on 3 June 1937 at the Château de Condé, and remained there in exile until their deaths.

WEDDED BLISS

These two views show the differences between weddings for the middle and working classes in the 1930s. Middle-class weddings (right) were society affairs, with long guest lists, whilst working-class weddings were smaller, with only a handful of guests. They often took place in registry offices because of the cost of hiring a church. Few couples could afford a honeymoon. It was quite common for newly married couples from poorer backgrounds to share the family home of either parents, until they could afford a house of their own.

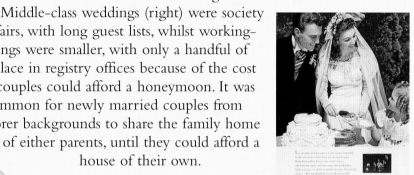

UNWANTED PREGNANCIES

Having babies when not married was disapproved of in the 1930s and 40s. However, many women, especially during the war, gave birth when they were still single. Some of these babies were brought up by the mother's parents as one of their own children. Some mothers were forced to place their babies in orphanages or to have them adopted. They usually had no contact with them again.

WARTIME ROMANCES

During the Second World War there were many sad goodbyes as husbands (and brothers and fathers, too) went off to war. There were also many joyful returns when the men returned on leave. Couples who might not have got together in peacetime had love affairs, and there seemed to be a lot of romance about.

WOMEN AND CHILDREN

IN THE FIRING LINE

A great deal of the work done in weapons factories was by women during the war. Some even joined the Women's Home Defence Corps and were trained to shoot anti-aircraft guns during air raids.

The Second World War allowed women to do much more than they had before. They took on many jobs that had only been open to men before the war, because most of the men were called up to serve. Women were also important within the armed services. They did not fight but worked in support roles. During the 1930s, there was a large improvement in infant and maternal death rates. In 1900 the number of babies who died at birth was around 142 per 1,000 births. By 1938 the figure had dropped to 55 deaths per 1,000 births. Maternal deaths (when the mother dies giving birth or soon after), fell from 6 to 3 per 1,000 between 1900 and 1938.

CHILDREN'S EDUCATION

The 1944 Education Act finally sorted out the problems of educating children. After that date, all children at both primary and secondary levels could receive free education. It also created a three-tier system of primary schools, secondary schools, and colleges of further education. The leaving age was 15. In 1940 a free school milk scheme was introduced to improve the health of children.

SIMPLE PLEASURES

Children were encouraged to be active in their play. They tended to make and find their own amusement. There were no clever electronic or computer games, and toys were usually quite simple, made of wood or lead. (Lead is now known to be poisonous and has been banned in toy production.)

WOMEN'S LAND ARMY

Many women signed up to join the 'Women's Land Army'. Often for city girls, this meant actually leaving home and living on a farm helping with the war effort to keep the nation fed. For this, women received £2.40 per week, of which about half was deducted for their board and lodging. The idea of a women's 'land army' had first been introduced during the First World War, and was reintroduced in the 1940s.

STREET WISE

In the towns and cities only a few people had gardens in the 1930s. Most working-class houses simply had a back yard with an outside lavatory. Most children had to play in the streets, as there were few playgrounds. Parks were formal and patrolled by park keepers, who did not allow children to play. With little traffic, the streets were seen as safe playgrounds.

INEQUALITY

Although women had been working in factories for the previous 200 years, they often had to do different work from men. The increase of female workers in the 1930s and 40s allowed them to work on equal terms with men, often performing the same jobs. They still did not however, receive the same pay. On average, men earned twice as much as women and, in some industries, even young boys earned more than women doing the same jobs.

SAVIOUR OF THE SKIES

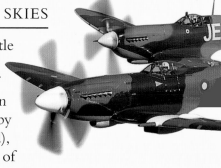

For most Britons, the turning point of the war was the Battle of Britain in 1940, which many considered was won by Spitfires, shown here. The Spitfire had a top speed of 579 km/h, and was easier to fly than the German Messerschmitt 109. The Royal Airforce (RAF) was helped by radar stations in south-east England (the first in the world), which provided British pilots with accurate early warning of approaching enemy aircraft.

HOME GUARD

In the early part of the war, Britain was protected by groups of volunteers who acted as air-raid wardens, fire-watchers and civil defence volunteers (later known as the Home Guard). They were made up of citizens who were unable to join the armed services. As well as defending the home shores, they were a great boost to the mood of the country.

THIS SPECIAL RESPIRATOR FOR A SMALL CHILD IS GOVERNMENT PROPERTY. ANY PERSON WHO HAS IT IN HIS POSSESSION IS RESPONSIBLE IN LAW FOR USING CARE TO KEEP IT IN GOOD CONDITION. IT IS TO BE RETURNED TO THE LOCAL AUTHORITY IN WHOSE AREA THE POSSESSOR MAY BE AT ANY TIME, EITHER ON REQUEST OR WHEN NO LONGER REQUIRED.

THE 'BLITZ'

Shortly after its defeat in the Battle of Britain, the German air force began a new series of mass-bombing raids, known as the *blitzkrieg* (or 'blitz') on British cities.
The first raid was on London on 8 September 1940, when 430 citizens died, 1,600 were seriously injured and many thousands made homeless. Many more raids followed, bringing chaos to Britain. One of the worst raids was on Coventry – centre of the British armaments industry, in November 1940 (shown here). In one night, a third of the city was destroyed and over 4,000 citizens killed.

WAR AND WEAPONS

The Second World War is thought to have been the worst war in history. It began in September 1939, when Germany invaded Poland. Britain and France were drawn into the war as Poland's allies against Germany. The fighting ended in August 1945. By then 40 million people had been killed and many more injured. In Britain a sense of community spirit developed for the first time, as everyone 'pulled together' to defeat the enemy.

RAISING MORALE

George VI took his role as wartime monarch very seriously. He made several morale-boosting visits to the troops, including to Egypt in 1943 (shown here). He even volunteered to accompany the allied invasion forces on D-Day 1944, but Prime Minister Winston Churchill thought it would be too dangerous.

THE WAR OF WARS

The Second World War did not just affect the soldiers fighting on the front line. For the first time, civilians (people who were not in the armed forces) became enemy targets. This not only lowered morale but also damaged the economy of the country. Germany launched mass-bombing raids in Britain, concentrating on London and the south, plus other industrial cities such as Coventry and Liverpool. Every family had to carry gas masks. Air-raid shelters made of corrugated iron and earth were built in gardens, too. Many children in London and the south-east were evacuated to safer, country areas. They stayed there until it was safe enough to return home.

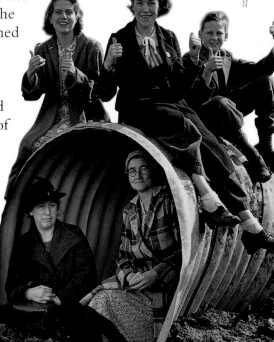

CRIME AND PUNISHMENT

oday the juvenile crime rate is rising, but in the 1930s this kind of crime was very rare. In 1938, in the whole of Britain, just 49 'juveniles' (aged 15-16) and 737 adolescents (aged 17-21) were sent to borstal. Most crimes (about 95 percent) were theft, especially at the end of the Second World War when most British troops were 'demobbed'. They returned home and were unable to find jobs. Basic items were hard to find, so some turned to crime just to survive.

JOHN CHRISTIE

John Christie (1898-1953), of 10 Rillington Place, London, was one of the worst serial killers of this century. Between 1943 and the early 1950s he murdered at least six women. He was eventually caught, tried and hanged in 1953.

PRISON LIFE

Britain's prison system could not cope with the sudden increase in the number of prisoners, (about 47,000 a year) after the Second World War. This picture shows new prisoners at Strangeways Prison, Manchester, 1948.

DEATH PENALTY

At the beginning of the 19th century over 200 crimes were punishable by death, including petty theft. By the 1930s this had been reduced to two: murder and treason. The punishment for all other serious crimes became long prison sentences. Crimes of treason have always been rare, but in 1946 William Joyce (otherwise known as Lord Haw-Haw) was hanged at Wandsworth for broadcasting anti-British propaganda during the Second World War.

THE BLACK MARKET

Perhaps because there was a 'common enemy', or because many young men were away fighting, there was a sense of 'community spirit' in Britain, and crime rates during the Second World War were the lowest on record. The most common crimes were smuggling and selling goods without ration coupons on the 'black market'. Many of these goods, including food and clothing, were stolen by people working in government supply centres.

ACID BATH MURDERER

John George Haigh (1909-49) was one of the most gruesome criminals of the 1940s, responsible for the death of several people, all murdered for their money. He disposed of his victims' bodies in a vat of acid, earning him the nickname the 'Acid Bath Murderer'. He is seen here leaving the court at Horsham during his trial. He was found guilty and hanged for his crimes in 1949.

POLICEMEN'S BEAT

During the 1930s and 40s the most familiar police activity was routine patrols. Their presence was often enough to deter many criminals. In the days before computer-based traffic control, the police often directed traffic at busy junctions, as shown left.

TRANSPORT AND SCIENCE

CLUES TO THE PAST

In 1947, Willard Libby developed a method of dating organic material by measuring the amount of radioactive carbon-14 it contained. Although it has limits, carbon dating has become one of the most widely used methods of dating artefacts and monuments such as Stonehenge (above).

There were many advances in science and technology in the 1930s and 40s. Frank Whittle developed the first successful jet engine in 1937. During the war years the engine was developed for fighter aircraft, but it was later adapted for other uses. Also during the war, an 'arms race' developed between Germany and the Allies. German scientists produced the V1 and V2 rockets (known as 'flying bombs') which travelled at speeds of 6,080 km/h. The advances made in rocket technology led to the American and Russian space programmes after the war. New materials developed at this time included aluminium, plastic and polythene.

COMMERCIAL AIRLINES

For those who could afford it, a new form of travel, by airliner, became available, greatly reducing travelling time. The first turbo-prop airliner – the Vickers Viscount – made its maiden flight in 1948.

NUCLEAR TECHNOLOGY

Once it was realized that the nucleus of an atom could be split (as shown below), scientists in Britain, America and Europe worked hard to develop nuclear technology quickly. Nuclear scientists (many who fled from Europe to America to escape the Nazis) developed the first atomic bombs that were dropped on Japan, and finally ended the Second World War. Apart from its use as a weapon, nuclear technology developed quickly after the war, especially in the field of energy.

THE CATSEYE™

The Catseye™ was invented by Percy Shaw in 1934. These small reflectors mounted into the road surface were lit up by car headlights. They helped reduce accidents at night and are still used today.

TRAMWAYS

The most common form of public transport in towns was the tram. Horse-drawn trams were introduced in the late 19th century and replaced in the 1930s with electric trams. They ran on rails laid in the roads, and had a rotor arm on the roof connected to overhead cables so they could get electricity to power their engines.

CYCLING

By the 1930s horse-drawn traffic was disappearing fast. For many, bicycles were the main form of transport, especially for getting to and from work. In pre-war Britain it is estimated there were about 10 million cyclists.

GETTING YOUR ANSWERS
...at electronic speed!

IBM INTERNATIONAL BUSINESS MACHINES

THE AGE OF THE COMPUTER

Early computers were huge machines. They were developed in 1947. Much slower than modern computers, they were mostly used for mathematical calculations.

CAR DESIGN

As new types of steel were developed in the 1930s and 40s, it became possible to design cars with curves, rather than the typical box-like construction of early models. By the end of the 1930s cars had most of the standard features that ours have today. Developments since then have largely been refinements and improvements.

RELIGION

During the 1930s there was a large drop in the number of people who went to church. Many, having lived through the Depression, began to change their values and think differently when the country began to recover. It was in the 1930s that mass media and entertainment were developed, and for the first time 'leisure' was run like a business. People started to spend more of their money on leisure. Many turned to gambling, hoping they would never have to experience the hardships of the Depression again.

The Church did not approve of this behaviour, and people began to turn away from organized religion.

THE HYPOCRISY OF WAR

The trend of turning away from the Church continued throughout the Second World War. Many who witnessed the horrors of war turned away from God for allowing such cruelty to happen. Most regiments had their own priest, but many thought they were hypocrites.

RASTAFARIAN SECT

In 1930 a new religious sect, the Rastafarians, emerged in Jamaica and spread throughout the West Indies and on to Britain. They reject 'white' culture and Christianity, but keep some, if not all, of the Bible. They take their name from Ras Tafari, Emperor of Ethiopia, regarded by many as God of the black race. It was one of several alternative religions that have evolved since the 1930s.

THE DEAD SEA SCROLLS

In 1947 an important religious discovery was made in Israel. A collection of manuscripts was found, written on papyrus and leather, and dating back to 200 BCE. They were found in caves at Qumran, near the Dead Sea (right), by some men who were looking for a lost goat. They form an almost complete collection of Old Testament writings. Some are written in code and contain some interesting variations to the Old Testament as we know it.

JEHOVAH'S WITNESSES

In 1931 the International Bible Students' Association changed its name to the Jehovah's Witnesses. Jehovah is the ancient Hebrew personal name for God. Followers give a percentage of their earnings to the movement. They believe, amongst other things, that they must convert as many people as possible to their beliefs in order to save the human race from self-destruction.

CHANGING TIMES

By 1948, the number of people going to Sunday service had declined. The Anglican Church suffered most. More people still attended chapel in Wales, the Presbyterian Church in Scotland and Catholic churches throughout the country.

GLOSSARY

Abdicated When a king or queen gives up their crown and chooses not to rule.

Black market A secret trade in items that were either illegal, or controlled. For example selling rationed items.

Demobbed The name given to troops coming out of the armed forces or returning home.

Hypocrites People who pretend to agree with moral beliefs which they do not follow themselves. For example army priests saying that killing is wrong.

Immunized Being made immune (not affected by) certain diseases.

Juvenile Young people below the age of normal criminal prosecution. Juveniles are treated differently to adult criminals and have special courts.

Reconstituted Dried food that has water added to it to make it complete. For example, dried potato is reconstituted when water is added to make instant mashed potato.

Sterile Making something free from bacteria. This is important in preventing diseases and infections after surgery.

Treason A very serious crime of betraying your country. This could be either by trying to kill the ruling monarch, or by trying to overthrow the government of the time.

ACKNOWLEDGEMENTS

We would like to thank: Graham Rich, Hazel Poole Rosie Hankin, and Elizabeth Wiggans for their assistance.
Copyright © 2008 ticktock Entertainment Ltd.
First published in Great Britain by *ticktock* Media Ltd., Unit 2, Orchard Business Centre, North Farm Road, Tunbridge Wells, Kent, TN2 3XF, UK.
All rights reserved. No part of this publication may be reproduced, stored in a retrieval system, or transmitted in any form or by any means electronic, mechanical, photocopying, recording or otherwise, without prior written permission of the copyright owner.
A CIP catalogue record for this book is available from the British Library.
ISBN 978 1 84696 660 6
Picture research by Image Select.
Printed in China.

Picture Credits:
t=top, b=bottom, c=centre, l=left, r=right, OFC=outside front cover, IFC=inside front cover, OBC=outside back cover, IBC=inside back cover

Arcaid; 16/17t. AKG; 16tl. Ann Ronan at Image Select; 16bl, 17tr. Robert Opie Collection; OFC (main pic), 2/3, 4cl, 6/7 & OFC, 7tr, 9br & OBC, 10/11t, 10/11b, 10/11, 11br, 12bl, 13tr, 14tl, 15c, 20tl & OBC, 23r & OFC, 24/25 & OBC, 29b & OFC, 28/29, 28cl, 28tr. The Advertising Archives; 4/5t, 6tl, 9tr, 12/13, 18c, 21tr, 27b & OFC, 29tr. The Bridgeman Art Library; 30/31ct. Hulton Deutsch; OFCtl, 3br, 4tl, 4/5, 7br, 6bl, 8tl , 9c, 9tl, 10bl, 10tl, 11c, 14bl, 15tr, 15t, 15br, 16/17, 19br, 20/21, 22/23t, 24l, 25tr, 25br & IFC, 26tl, 29tl, 29c, 30/31ct, 31b. Hulton Getty; 2tl, 2bl, 3, 5cr, 5br, 6cl, 7bl, 8b, 12br, 13cr, 14/15, 18/19, 18bl, 20bl, 20/21ct, 21cr, 22tl, 22cl, 26b, 27c, 31tr, 30tl. Image Select; 11tr, OFC & 32, 18/19, 28tl, 28bl. Telegraph Colour Library; 30bl. Aviation Photographs International; 24tr. PIX S.A;18tl, 22/23c. Victoria & Albert Museum; 12tl, 22b, OFC & OBC.

Every effort has been made to trace the copyright holders and we apologize in advance for any unintentional omissions.
We would be pleased to insert the appropriate acknowledgement in any subsequent edition of this publication.